Letter from Tokyo

Letter from Tokyo

Anthony Thwaite

HUTCHINSON

London Melbourne Auckland Johannesburg

© Anthony Thwaite 1987

All rights reserved

This edition first published in 1987 by Hutchinson Ltd,
an imprint of Century Hutchinson Ltd, Brookmount House,
62–65 Chandos Place, London WC2N 4NW

Century Hutchinson Australia Pty Ltd
PO Box 496, 16–22 Church Street, Hawthorn,
Victoria 3122, Australia

Century Hutchinson New Zealand Ltd,
PO Box 40-086, Glenfield, Auckland 10, New Zealand

Century Hutchinson South Africa (Pty) Ltd
PO Box 337, Bergvlei, 2012 South Africa

Photoset by Rowland Phototypesetting Ltd
Bury St Edmunds, Suffolk
Printed and bound in Great Britain by
The Gurnsey Press Co. Ltd,
Gurnsey, Channel Islands

British Library Cataloguing in Publication Data

Thwaite, Anthony
    Letter from Tokyo.
    I. Title
    821'.914   PR6070.H9

    ISBN 0 09 170551 7

for Ann and for Alice

Contents

Notes and Acknowledgements

With the exception of 'Soseki', an earlier version of which was written in England in 1983, all the poems in Parts I and II of this book were written during an extended stay in Japan in 1985–86. Three of the poems in Part III were also written in Japan. I am deeply indebted to the Japan Foundation for granting me a one-year Fellowship attached to the University of Tokyo, giving me time to write. I am also indebted to my sponsors for that Fellowship, Shinsuke Ando, Yasunari Takahashi, and Derek Brewer; to Hisaaki Yamanouchi and Reiko Yamanouchi, for their company on many journeys, and for much else; and to Hiro Ishibashi, for a great deal of encouragement and generosity.

Some of these poems were first broadcast by the BBC, and published in: *Encounter*, the *Listener*, the *Literary Review*, the *London Magazine*, the *Mainichi Daily News*, *Mandeville Press*, *Observer*, *P.N. Review*, *Poetry Book Society Supplements* 1980, 1982 and 1984, *Rialto*, *Spectator*, *The Times Literary Supplement*. 'Two Poets' was the result of a commission by the Tate Gallery. The 'Five Occasions' were originally published as follows: 'The Mole at Kilpeck Church' in *Grigson at Eighty* (Rampant Lions Press, 1985); 'Second After Trinity' in *Between Comets: for Norman Nicholson at 70* (Taxus Press, 1984); 'Cold Comforts' in *A Garland for the Laureate: poems presented to Sir John Betjeman on his 75th birthday* (Celandine Press, 1981); 'For Roy Fuller at Seventy' in *Poems for Roy Fuller on his seventieth birthday* (Sycamore Press, 1982); 'A Sort of Ballade for a Sort of New Hero' in the *Poetry Book Society Supplement*, 1984.

Part I

Letter from Tokyo

This season of spring/summer/autumn/winter is treacherous.
Please be vigilant of your fragile health throughout it.

My garden is only the size of a cat's forehead.
This is because my fees are a sparrow's tears.

You are welcome to visit me whenever you wish,
Though the squalor of my abode will shock your feet.

Your handsome frame undoubtedly will suffer
From submitting to the rabbit-hutch I inhabit.

Perhaps when spring/summer/autumn/winter succeed in their
  courses
I may trouble you with another communication.

My command of your language is, you will see, defective.
Can you understand my poor meaning? That is remarkable.

A Word of Advice

This is a holy place. It is not a hotel.
You are guests, true, but also pilgrims.

Here we eat no flesh or fish: it is well
Two of you already follow this rule.

You must follow our other rules, including the times
Baths must be taken, the dimming of lights,
And the extinguishing of talk.
Gongs will be sounded to let you know of these things.

We expect you to consume whatever you are given –
Give thanks for it, and always abhor waste.

The hangings on the walls, which you cannot read,
Are prayers and reminders of prayer.

You seem unenlightened. You will, I hope, not stay long.
Something about you disturbs the atmosphere:
I noticed you smiling as if in doubt
Whether this was quite the place the guidebook described.

I am the bride of the priest. I do not smile.

My manner may seem unfriendly. It is not so intended.
Simply, you must accept.
                                    And remember
This is a holy place. It is not a hotel.

Abroad Thoughts from Abroad

Mozart on NHK, *The Messiah* in Shinjuku,
Cinzano cold in the hand, fragrant in the mouth:
I am a citizen of the world, and so are they.

On Wednesday we shall continue with Sylvia Plath,
On Thursday the undergraduates
Will attend my lecture on Hopkins and Kipling.

People in England send us Christmas cards
With jokes about holly festooning the 'crispy noodles'.
Daft. We can even buy Marmite quite easily.

In the street, I avoid the eyes of foreigners,
Who in any case are few and far between.
Being abroad, why should we mix together?

I am a citizen of the world, and so are they,
And so are the students drifting under the window
Giggling about something or other in Japanese.

This is an ironical poem about happiness.
I am as happy as I could ever be.
The Japanese say they do not understand irony.

Kanji

As I walk I notice the shapes of characters
Bold on shop-signs, on the indicators of buses,
On the covers of magazines, on the doorposts of houses.

Some I know, and say to myself quietly.
Others I recognise, understand, but can't remember
What sound they make. Many I recognise
But cannot understand. And many more
Always seem new, unknown.

Ya, valley, is like a little house
But often pronounced in quite another way.
I is a well, but looks like a word-game's grid.
Ishii is stone – a quarry-block, chisel above.
Kawa (or *gawa*) is easy – a river with banks.

But three horizontal strokes need puzzling out –
The numeral three, but spoken sometimes as *san*,
Sometimes as *mitsu*, and no indication which.

A rice-paddy, or a field, is a cross in a square,
Called *da* or *ta*: an entrance a different square,
Or it may be an exit.

So it goes on, as I walk. I am learning to read
Like a child, an illiterate, adding and adding
Here a new shape, and there a new sound, and sometimes
Shape, sound, and sense together.
                                        But it is too late.
I sit in the bus and watch a ten-year-old turning
Page after page of characters, reading them all,
Not noticing what he is doing, simply becoming
Someone who knows: leaving me learning, alone.

Cicadas in Japan

Hearn heard them, and thought them magical,
Tried to distinguish
The multiple trills and screechings, different
From decibels in Italy or Provence:
Shrill carapace of shellac, trembling membranes
Strumming glum cacophonies.

And they are indeed alien, their quavers
Underline again
And yet again how different they, and we, are –
Like the nightingale that is not a nightingale,
The crow that will never be a crow,
Though sweet, though raucous.

And yet, in the swelter of summer, in a thick sweat,
Why not different?
They go with the twilight, the night, the day, the dawn
Coming again in shrill loudspeaker vans
Announcing news I cannot understand,
Speaking in tongues, wheezing out miracles.

Music To My Ears

A language to be learned, like any other,
Absorbed in childhood without knowing how,
Simply exposed to it and beating time
Before we read it, if we ever read it.

But it has rarer forms, has dialects
Unheard until a samisen's nervous strum
Plucks at the ears' plectrum, or a missing thud
Expected on a drum tells us its rules
Are not our rules. A single quivering string
Excites the desert, or a quavering howl
Means long-lost beauty to another's ear:

Barbarian gibberish to an audience
That has never heard the other harmonies
Other feet tap to, deaf to other tunes.

Shrine

Postures that are not dances; chants
That weld together words that are not words;
Drum, flute and bells making a kind of music
That is not music – shuddering, then still,
Then moving at a steady rhythmic pace
Under an almost mindless tuneless tune.

These negatives betray their ignorance:
Things that are not imply that something is.
Beyond the postures, chants, drum, flute and bells,
Beyond the celebrants, behind a screen,
Something is hidden in the sanctuary
Locked in a box no one has ever seen.

Shock

An easing of walls,
A shuddering through soles:
A petal loosens, falls.

In the room, alone:
It begins, then it has gone.
Ripples outlast stone.

Rain-smell stirs the heart;
Nostrils flare. A breath. We wait
For something to start.

The flavour of fear,
Something fragile in the air.
Gone, it remains here.

Dawn in Zempukuji

Phlegmatic hawkings, stertorous plummetings –
Our Chinese neighbour through the bedroom wall
Reaches for virtue from her tubes and lungs,
And serenades each dawn and dusk, her call
Shaking the frail partition. Then there comes
A genuine tremor like a roll of drums.

Birdcalls begin, unrecognised. Soft rain
Sifting through leaves, tapping through guttering.
Clatter of wooden sandals. At the pane
A moth is trapped in mesh, is fluttering
Against my pillow. Up through jets of dreams
Another tremor, then another, comes.

Variations on *Seki*

Look for the radical. Establish context.
If necessary, magnify the sign.
Use of the syllabary script may help.
The homophone is frequent. Now read on.

A most decisive battle. Build a dam.
Lose by a whisker. Neptune's revel. Pink.
Man of profound learning. Budgerigar.
A cough. The spine. Dead silence. Barren land.
Wages of sin. Stone pillar. Wipe the slate.
One-eyed. Red Army. Rice steamed with red beans.
Impromptu drawing. Evil of long standing.
Here. Bygone days. Put out of countenance.
Stark naked. Snowdrifts. One-armed person. Load.
Responsibility. The best one can expect.

O interlocking mesh of stroke and brush –
A web of dew which no sun clarifies:
Thesaurus of small treasure-houses, locked
Against the outsider, the illiterate.

Patterns

There is a word for the pattern in things –
The grain in bamboo, the markings in jade,
The lie of an animal's fur, strands in a thread.
Each has its quiddity of patternings,
And none can fade.

There is an order. There is a fixed place
Established within the pattern. The prince
Speaks only within his rank. It is a dance
Where each must put a mask before his face.
We must convince

The gruff barbarian that he cannot play
This skilful game, or even learn the rules:
Our scholars know his blundering reason fails
Trapped in the torments of the only Way
Taught in our schools.

They cannot penetrate our subtleties,
Our precepts of the Gods and of the shapes
Taken by the divinity that slips
Between us; between our divinities
And theirs – mere tropes,

Approximate translations, figures flicked
Inaccurately on a counting-frame.
Ours is a pattern flowing down a stream,
Not to be caught, a language none inflect
And none can tame.

The Court Examination

In this time of lack of wisdom
When the turbulence of all things
Threatens harmony and order,
We shall now propose conundrums
To the Ministers and Princes,
And afterwards give prizes
To those who give wise answers.

In this year a serpent and a dog copulated. Presently they both died together. If conception had occurred, what would have been the result?

The stinking leeks
In the fields of millet,
The roots and shoots of them
We shall strike down,
Sang the soldiers of Kumé,
The valiant soldiers.

Stones disappear beneath the surface of the earth, great trees wither away, saplings take their place. Where are there trustworthy memorials of events a millennium ago?

The pungent pepper
That grows in the hedges
Fire on our tongues,
We shall strike down,
Sang the soldiers of Kumé,
The valiant soldiers.

At the time when Heaven and Earth were not yet entirely separated, a certain thing was produced between them. It was in form like a reed-shoot. It became transformed into a god. What was the name of this deity?

And those who creep round
The sea-rock of Isé,
Creeping like sea-snails,
We shall strike down,
Sang the soldiers of Kumé,
The valiant soldiers.

The contest is now over,
The answers all examined.
It is clear that ancient wisdom
No longer dwells among you.
Let the Ministers and Princes
Be bound in hemp and rice-straw.
Let the soldiers have their way.

Sideshows
at the Tori-no-Ichi

She is quite pretty, young, and she swallows fire.
Her kimono has a special bib to protect her.
She mops her mouth with tissues daintily
In preparation for the plume of flame.

After she has done the necessary – a conflagration
Sucked down her throat and belched with a roar upwards –
Our attention is drawn to a writhing sack of snakes.
She is handed one snake, which she smoothes like a length of string.

Then, with a steady hand, the snake's head is inserted
Between her lips; she inhales, and it disappears
Along with four inches of body. The drumming increases.
The body withdraws, headless. She frowns and chews,

Opens her mouth, allows a trickle of blood
To flow down her chin, and wipes it gently away.
She has swallowed the snake's head. She smiles at the joke.
She mops her mouth with tissues daintily.

*   *   *

She is three feet tall, her head and trunk are those
Of a woman of sixty; but her arms are short and muscled
Like an infant Hercules, and her legs are stumps
Wrapped in bright rags, taffeta sausages.

She plays with a saucer balanced on a stick
Which she twirls in time to the music. By her side
Is a life-sized head of a puppet. She puts her own head
On the floor, and raises her trunk with a flip of her wrists.

But something is wrong with the tape-recorder.
It should be giving her something to dance to,
With the puppet's head stuck in her crotch and her tiny stumps
Waving like arms though they are really legs.

An assistant is called for, a big young capable man
Who fiddles with switches and knobs. But the tape-recorder
Refuses to play the game. The crowd is waiting.
They have paid their money and are waiting for something to happen.

But nothing happens. Till the three-foot woman shrugs
With her massive shoulders, and begins to move,
Waving her ragged legs, jiggling the puppet's head
In time to nothing, in a silent dance.

Osorezan
for Hisaaki Yamanouchi

Hell's various images, each labelled, mapped.

Scurfed shed-skin puddles,
Blood-pools and litter mixed,
Beaches of leprous rock,
Contusions of sand stained blue with votive coins,
Sulphurous stink drifting across dunes,
Eroded Buddhas roguish in red bibs:
And everywhere the pebbles to the dead
Inscribed, heaped up forever, scattered, piled
High for the billion foetuses aborted,
Now lost in Hell, who cannot reach the bridge
So close, so crimson, that leads to Paradise.
Frantic toy plastic windmills whirr above the cairns,
Rasping against the rooks' raw sniggering,
Chanting their sutras to the sanctuary
Here where we kneel and catch the priest's response,
Dead faded photographs, old cast-off clothes
Cluttering the beams with passed-on images
Of the known dead, those who were born and died,
A thousand years of shrined and shriving guilt,
Precise, clear, poignant, terrible, banal.

Hell is well mapped, but Paradise is not.

Hiroshima
August 1985

No way to deal with it, no way at all.
We did not have to come, and yet we came.
The things we saw were all the very same
As we expected. We had seen them all:
The fabric pattern printed on the skin,
The shadow of a body on a wall.
What wrapped our bodies round was much too thin.

Voyeurs, but sensitive not to display
Unseemly horror; yet sensing that we felt
Horror was here, and everywhere was shown.
We knew the arguments the other way –
If they had had the thing, it would have blown
Some other city, one of ours, away.
Was it guilt, shame, fear, nausea that we smelt?

Self-accusations, bewilderment, disgust:
Those dripping rags of flesh, that faceless head,
The sky wiped black, the air crammed black with dust,
City of ghosts, museum of the dead.
No way to deal with it, no way at all.
We did not have to come, and yet we came.
The things we saw were all the very same
As we expected. We had seen them all.

Joshidaimae

That thin, sweet, pure cry
Like a hymn to the lost gods
Echoing over the traffic

At last comes into view:
A battered truck, its back
A banged-together oven,

Jerking between the gleaming
Nissans and Toyotas.
On this cold, brilliant day,

Crisp leaves falling like money,
The smell of roast sweet potatoes
Wafts from the glowing embers.

No one seems to want them.
Over the fortunate city
The January sun

Hands down magnificence
To the traffic-jams and the truck
And that thin, sweet, pure cry.

At the Fox Shrine

On the last day of the year at the fox shrine
I lit a candle. It blew out
Among the red banners and broken figurines
In a rubble of leaves and votives by a tree root.

I had found the candle, unlit, in all that mess,
Put my lighter to it, set it in a dish
Before the kitsch foxes. The first breeze
Extinguished the flame, before I could even wish –

Whatever it was I wished. Today was the wrong day
To come to the shrine: tomorrow the new year
Would bring out the crowds to scatter their coins and pray.
Today there was no one else there.

The hill path, the tall midwinter trees
Holding on to themselves, the late sun,
Were all indifferent to calendars,
To choosing a day for faith or superstition.

Whatever whim or instinct made me light
The candle at the tree root by the shrine,
The night ahead would blow the old year out,
Wind rising through deserted cypress and pine.

Sasuke no Inari, Kamakura

Part II

'Voices Through Clouds'

Kirishitan Monogatari
Three Last Words

I
1620

Even my name is doubtful – Fabian,
Fabian Fukansai, Fukansai Habian,
Fabian Fucan, Fabian Unguio . . .
A Japanese chameleon, on whose skin
All patterns slide in reformation; judged
Most promising of novices, apt
Pupil, master of tongues and argument,
Worst of inquisitors. In sophistry
You will not find my equal: I am there
With scruple, nicety, and forked contempt,
With casuistry, logic, and the knife
That lets just blood enough to keep you hale
But not enough to kill you. I am there
Above you in the pit, or battened down
Mired in your crouching cage, or in the fire,
Or on the cross. And, last, I am still there
When you cry out in your apostasy,
My mirror-image, Father Christopher,
Whose name blurs also as my name is blurred:
Henceforth *Sawano Chuan*, held in thrall,
Fellow-inquisitor, balked of martyrdom.

II
1636

Behind this mask I hear you, Fabian:
Twenty years fruitlessly, barbarian
Reformed in religion, I staggered in the faith.
Now, in the thirteenth year of Kan'ei,
Transmuted, purged, pure adherent of Zen,
With the Dragon constellations set in heaven,
I embrace my death. I hear the sentences
Read out from chronicles that will banish me.

'He was three days in the pit, and died a martyr.'

35

'As one falls, another rises:
As one deserts, another bears the Crown.'

In seething waters, above bubbling turds
Suspended, O my God: trussed, should I trust
That crookèd path, perverse and cursèd faith,
Those cross-yoked words –
Deceit Disclosed, Deus Destroyed, my God?
Out of the pit I cried, out of the dust,
Thy barbarous martyr, pleading for his death,
Printed in tears, gasped out with strangled breath.

'He bore a heavy cross, and down his back streamed
    blood.'

'The blood of the martyrs is the seed of the Church.'

Bateren Christopher, *Sawano Chuan*,
Superior turned renegade and spy,
I, the Apostate, knew three properties –
Of Man to sin, of Christian to repent,
Of Devil to perform the crime again
And yet again. This was my Trinity.
But these three now – blood, brocade, and gold,
The Cross, Christ's uniform, the weight of wealth,
The dazzling finery whose fruit is death –
I cast them off, and am come back to life,
Parodic resurrection, purged and shriven,
My eyes turned stalwartly away from Heaven.

III
1639

In the days of the Emperor Go-Nara, long ago,
The conch-nosed giant, eyes as big as saucers,
Stepped from the ship of Namban, screeched like an owl –
The long-clawed *Bateren*, the goblin breed.

At Sumiyoshi, by the sacred shrine,
There fell down at that footfall, in a flash,
Sixty-six pine trees, prophecy that all
Our provinces would topple at this tread,
This mouse-grey monster, wings spread like a bat.

Into our lord's presence came, bearing gifts:
Ten muskets, spectacles for near-and-far,
An insect-net fanned out huge as a hall
(Yet, folded, snug to fit a perfume-flask),
Picture-scrolls, medicines, goats, Cathay dogs,
Bolt after bolt of tawny russet cloth
(Pelts of orang-outang) – all bribes, all beads
Spangled with secrecies, with cruciforms –
Image of Deus hanging on the cross,
Virgin and Mother, womb besmirched with blood.

Thus the old stories . . . After *Bateren*
Came many *Furaten*, still goblin breed,
Still loaded with their baubled bric-à-brac,
But these wandered the streets enticingly
Curing the lepers, wretches poxed with boils,
Carbuncles, mange; beggars harelipped and lame,
Morons and menials, misfits and good-for-naughts.
These *Furaten*, too, concocted plots,
Pernicious mischief-work, deluded news,
Until our lord the Taiko took his stand –
Purged them, expelled them, drove them from our land.

Twenty-six criminals, their noses slit,
Dragged through the city streets: along the way
Gazed at the sky, looked for a miracle
Across the mountains – but no drop of dew
Succoured them then, or ever.
                              By the shore

37

In Nagasaki they were crucified,
Joining their Jesu (Jizo mockery).
Their bodies rotted on the crosses, both
Bodies and crosses pilfered secretly –
Believers' trophies, crosses and bones and skulls,
Each scrap of bone, each toothpick stick of wood
Traded as relics, holy amulets.

But we had let the sawdust out of them,
Weevils and termites, filthy predators,
Stews of unheard-of things from barbarous lands,
The flowered words that strew the Devil's path.

This is the Land of Gods, a tripod based
Sturdily on three legs: the Royal Sway,
The Way of the Gods, the Buddha's Path – let one
Be broken off, then sun and moon fall down,
The lantern lost which lights the gloomy night.

The Empire is at peace, tranquil the land:
A sainted reign, a golden age indeed.

> Completed
> here
> on a propitious day:
> eighth month of Kan'ei 16

Letters from Jakarta: 1641 and 1680

> Morning in spring, the fourth month:
> But here are no spring flowers.
> Nothing the same here
> Except for sunlight and moonlight.
> O how I miss Japan —
> If I could but see it again!

> So far, by so many leagues
> Of ocean, it keeps its distance —
> Yamato, out of my mind
> Never, sleeves wet with my tears.
> Why was my father foreign?
> How long since I left my home?

As you know, every year (thanks to the benevolence of the magistrates of Nagasaki) I have been able to receive letters and gifts. Last year (owing to the fortunate opportunities offered by a Dutch 'black ship' and the Chinese vessel) I have, as I confirm here, received letters and gifts twice. I am very grateful for all this . . .

> Exiled when just fourteen,
> Yet it seems yesterday
> When I hastily packed a few clothes,
> Went weeping, bewildered, on
>   board,
> Took leave of my nurse, my friends,
> Saw the coastline ebb away.

Now I entrust the following gifts of my own to you, through the good offices of the foreign captain. You will find them thus: 94 rolls of undyed cotton cloth, all rolled in one. One chest containing: three pounds of carrots (finest quality); two rolls of satin in light indigo; six rolls of calico; three rolls of deep green cloth tinted with yellow . . .

Writing like this, the ink
Is blurred and runs with my tears.
How you will think I have changed!
Dear one, please send me some seeds
Of oak and cedar and broom,
Some pine-cones, and incense-sticks –

Things to remind me of home,
Unchanging if I have changed.
All I can send you myself
Is this sash embroidered with flowers –
But they are the wrong flowers:
The home ones I have forgotten.

. . . a measure of woollen cloth better than any imported by the Dutch; four rolls of printed cotton; a single roll of twilled silk in black; a single roll of figured satin in black; a small assortment of sewing needles. All these for Kifu, wife of Shichiroemon, in Shimabara: she waited on me ever since she was a child, and I feel sorry for her in many ways.

Please do not laugh at me;
And if others do, you must tell them
The pattern is fanciful.
How could I ever forget,
As I have, those colours and shapes . . .
The years, the distance, the years.

As for the saké I have ordered this time, please deliver it to a man called Karu, in Dejima, in a double-barrelled cask, just in time for sailing. Unless this is done just in time, the saké might be stolen by the casual dock-workers.

Lonely, my life, and sad.
My inkstone overbrims
As I think of the yellow rose
You gave me in full bloom.
Now it has long withered.
Like dew, I must go too.

Though I live in this far land,
I pray that you won't forget me:
For even the briefest moment –
Like a flash of lightning over
The full-eared rice-fields of autumn –
I shall never forget you.

If I want anything, I shall let you know. Unless I ask for something, it is unnecessary. I only want chrysanthemums. The plants you sent me last year have all died, probably because I made too much fuss over them. Tender shoots and grafted scions would root here: say, one of crimson and the other variegated.

O how I miss Japan –
If I could but see it again!

Last year you tried sending me some potted Japanese radishes, but they seem to have got lost, either on board the ship or after they were landed. But in any case all such vegetables are easily available here at any time of the year. As for fruit, we lack nothing. The *Capitão* in Dejima is someone whom we have always looked upon as if he had been our own relative. I entrust everything, including this message, to him.

O how I miss . . .

Very sincerely yours,
Oharu (widow of Shinmosu)

41

On Dejima: 1845

A turn around the yard, then back again:
A pint of gin, a game of dice, to bed

Knocked out, locked in. Twenty-two exiled men
Marooned like ghosts who do not know they're dead.

Krieger talks rubbish. Blomhoff wants a whore
And says so, endlessly. Van Puyck adds up

Consignment figures for the umpteenth time.
Wail of a shakuhachi from the shore.

Tomorrow night, some fiefling in to sup:
Adam the cook prepares a fishy slime

Fit for outlandish palates, and sweet wine
To tilt his brains indulgently our way

('Your eminence, do take another cup') –
Turn a blind eye to Rahder's escapade

Last week (a scuffle on the landward side,
A bloody nose or two): we cover up

For one another like a gang of boys,
Distrust and honour shiftily in turn

Keeping the balance. Distantly, a noise
Of drum and cymbals marking out some rite

Pickled in superstition. Candles burn
Down to each dish, spit smoke, and then go out.

The hills of Nagasaki ring the night,
Our dark horizon where we cannot go.

Each day creeps by, each minute labours slow.
A hundred years from now, perhaps some light

Will fall upon this heathen harbour town –
But let the gin take over, let me row

My numbed, thick, sleepy body out to sea.
Let me go easy. Let me sink and drown

Far from this fan-shaped offshore prison where
Seabirds screech alien words in alien air.

The Envoys: 1860

Over the Western sea hither from Niphon come,
Courteous, the swart-cheek'd two-sworded envoys,
Leaning back in their open barouches, bare-headed,
    impassive . . .
Florid with blood, pensive, rapt with musings, hot with passion,
Sultry with perfume, with ample and flowing garments,
With sunburnt visage, with intense soul and glittering eyes.

Walt Whitman

Grey-pink and shining flowers look down on us –
Thousands of faces peering from high windows.
The faces become flowers, we are showered with them,
The horses and the carriages strewn with blossoms
As we go on down valleys of tall buildings
To such wild shouts, to such wild thundering music!
Dismounting from our carriages, we step
Into the Congress, watch from a balcony
Members brandishing their fists as if in temper –
Speeches at tops of voices, all excited, unexplained.
Then the Smithsonian, pickled snakes, men's bodies
Pickled also, a vast display of hair-specimens
Cut from successive Presidents – disgusting to exhibit
The hair of dead men in a public place. But worse
That evening – men and bareshouldered women glued together
Hop round the floor to music: we are told
This is a 'dance', and that all classes (rich, poor, young, old)
Enjoy this pastime – the women's waists encircled
As if in copulation. Exploding liquors – champagne –
Then, arm in arm, each of us takes a lady
To face a banquet . . . Rice fried in butter, rice
Sprinkled with sugar, emetic dishes spread on tablecloths
White as a field of snow. And Morita
Drinks from his fingerbowl in ignorance . . .

We are the first Ambassadors, our Government
And people anxiously await our safe return.
We came to secure the Treaty, not for pleasure
(Though pleasure may be had from careful inspection

44

Of certain instruments, engines, maps, machines,
Rifles and pistols of the latest make).
Kindnesses shown are but seldom pleasures:
How often, to our shame, we bow, refuse, parrot the phrase
'Excuse us – it is not our country's custom'!

Washington, Philadelphia, New York –
We droop from so much travel, so much boisterousness
Battering our ears with unintelligible whoops,
Such heat weighing us down in robes designed
For simpler, gentler ways – for dignity
Hard to adhere to in such rough-and-tumble.
Democracy – Liberty – The Open Door –
A barrier without ceremony through which
Millions as yet unborn must push and jostle
Because of what we were sent to do, have done,
Cordial with gifts, received with gratitude,
Uncertain as the blossom that looks down
Poised for a moment, whether to stay or fall,
Destined to fall, now looking down on us,
Dissolving into faces, grey-pink, shining,
That stare at us in dreams that do not fade.

Of Japan at Ten Hours' Sight: 1889

– Whence the camphor and the lacquer and the shark-skin swords
   all come:
We shall stop at Nagasaki; on to Kobé northwards; then
By clockwork engine ticking by paddies, mountains, shrines,
To the Emperor's new capital spread out around the bay.

*   *   *

A tea-girl in fawn-coloured crêpe under a cherry tree:
Behind, green pines, two babies, and a hog-backed bridge that
   spans
A river (coloured bottle-green) and boulders (coloured blue);
In front, a little policeman in a badly-fitting suit.

Their language is a patter of no tone or weight or stress,
Their poetry is syllables on the fingers of one hand,
Without rhythm, with no rhymes at all – and what it seems to say
Is that seasons change and blossoms fall and nothing stays the same.

Their music is a squawk of strings and a rumble on a drum,
Their songs a caterwauling through a set of blackened teeth,
Their plays are Henry Irving guyed by drunken undergrads –
The howls and jerks and colours of a puppet on a string.

*   *   *

In a workshop like a fairy's house sit men and girls and boys,
Neat and proper in surroundings, with an iris by the pond:
They lift their eyes from painting on Satsuma with a brush
To gaze at sprigs of cherry or a pine against the sky.

We, the nation of glass flower-shades and the pink-puce worsted
   mat,
Red-green puppy-dogs in china, poisonous Brussels
   carpet-lengths,
Now presume to lecture haughtily on Art and Craft and Taste
To the humble yellow people of the Islands of the Dawn.

Bog-trotting Briton, blundering in among the porcelain,
New York Professor, blathering sententiousness through cigars –
Have you noticed (as you duck your head to go into a room)
What has happened, and is happening, and will happen ere you rise?

All the skittles we have played with for six hundred years and more
They have picked up in an instant, they have learned the Book of
    Rules,
They listen when we tell them things they've known since Time
    began,
But patiently, so patiently, they wait for what they don't.

We taught them engineering, we sold them lovely guns,
We gave them fine roast-beef to eat, and whisky by the quart,
The civilized black bowler, the most advanced white spats,
Corkscrews, penknives, stucco, Worcester Sauce – a Constitution,
    too.

Their women are like little dolls, their children dolls of dolls,
Their laughter is the tinkle of a thousand tiny bells.
Their cavalry is comic, their infantry a joke . . .
But they waited till they wanted us; and what they want is All.

*   *   *

This people is a question-mark, and a puzzle to the head:
Such babu-ways, such stick-at-it, such comic-tragic squints . . .
Yet they know what they are after, and they'll drop us smartly when
The tooth of their desire picks clean the bone of ignorance.

I have dreamed of foreign monsters come to life in fairyland.
I have seen the writing on the wall, scratched on the panelled gold:
Madame Blavatsky smoking 'neath the Nikko ginkgo trees,
And Mister Caine, MP, denouncing saké as a sin.

47

The Jap is not a native, nor a sahib, but an odd
Sort of hybrid of the species – Chink, French, German, Hottentot,
With a dash of Yank and Redskin – but under all the lot
He's a warrior, and an artist, and a Jappo through and through.

I weep to see the hybrid, I anticipate the man
Who in time will whip the Chinaman, the Muscovite, and all;
For the day is fast approaching when the Rising Sun will fly
Over Manchu Palace, Onion-Dome – and maybe on Big Ben.

*   *   *

We are sailing out from Tokyo, from the edge of fairyland:
I can hear the baby bugles blowing bravely in my head,
I can see the tiny horses with their midgets on the strand –
And no one now can tuck the toys back in their tiny bed.

Soseki
(London: December 1902)

A lost dog slinking through a pack of wolves.

Sour yellow droplets frozen on each branch,
The tainted breath of winter in the fog:
Coal-smells, and cooking-smells (meat-fat, stewed-fish),
And smells of horse-dung steaming in the streets:
Smoke groping at the windowpanes, a stain
Left hanging by the mean lamp where I trace
Page after page of Craig's distempered notes . . .

     Winter withering
     Autumn's last scattering leaves:
     London is falling.

I want a theory, a science with firm rules
Plotting the truth objectively through all these infinite spaces.
I look out of the window over the whitened blankness,
And from the East the moon lights up half the river.

But it is hallucination: cab-lights from Clapham Common
Flash at the pane, my head throbs over the little fire,
I am crying in the darkness, my cheeks sticky with tears.
Far, far beyond the heavens the forms of departing clouds . . .

Downstairs, those sisters plot and scheme together –
I found the penny on the windowsill,
The one I gave the beggar yesterday. Ridiculous pity,
Sly instruments of torture!
                 'Natsume's mad' –
That telegram sent home by Okakura –
Will they believe it? Is it so? Is he my friend?
I have no friends. By the light of the dying fire
I underscore these lines, and more, and more . . .

     December evening.
     Light at the window shining.
     Something in hiding.

London is districts learned from Baedeker
And learned on foot. England is somewhere else.
A day in Cambridge seeing Doctor Andrews,
The Dean of Pembroke, offering me sherry.
Too many 'gentlemen' – at Oxford too.
Someone said *Edinburgh*, but the speech up there
Is northern dialect, *Tohōku*-style.
So London it must be – the Tower, its walls
Scrawled with the dying words of men condemned:
Lodgings in Gower Street with Mrs Knot;
That vast Museum piled with pallid Greeks;
West Hampstead, and then Camberwell New Road . . .
I measure out the metres as I walk,
Finding sad poetry in the names of places.

Sometimes, walking the streets thronged with such tall and
    handsome ones,
I see a dwarf approaching, his face sweaty – and then
I know it for my own reflection, cast back from a shop-window.
I laugh, it laughs. 'Yellow races' – how appropriate.

'Least poor Chinese' – I think I hear – or 'Handsome Jap' . . .
Sneers of a group of labourers, seeing me go by
In frock-coat, top-hat, parody of 'English gentleman'
Sauntering down King's Parade or in the High . . .
I walk to Bloomsbury, walk back to Clapham,
Carry my Meredith or Carlyle through the drizzle,
Munching with difficulty a 'sandwich' on a bench in the park
Soaked by the rain, buffeted by the wind . . .

Far, far beyond the heavens the forms of departing clouds,
And in the wind the sound of falling leaves.

It is time to be deliberate, to use
Such gifts as I am given, to escape
The traveller's to-and-fro, the flow of facts
Unchecked, to make a system that will join
Blossom to branch, reason to intuition,

Wave after wave uniting as each falls
Under the next that follows up the beach . . .

> A cry outside shakes
> The tangle of waterpipes:
> Midnight: a mouse squeaks.

A frightened mouse in a cell facing north,
I have almost forgotten what brought me here
Or what I do from day to day.
                              I know
I sat with Craig for an hour this morning,
Hearing him mumbling Shakespeare through his beard,
Gave him my shillings in an envelope
Bound round with ribbon which he plucked away
Impatiently and mannerless – due fee
For pedagogic drudgery. So walked back,
Wondering could I afford a mess of eggs
In the cabby-shelter out in Battersea,
And settled for a farthing bun and 'tea'
Scabby with milk served in a cracked white mug
At the stall by Wandsworth Bridge. Such humdrum things
To maze the mind and clog the intellect . . .

By the old castle at Komoro
The clouds are white and the wanderer grieves.

Impenetrable people, country bumpkins,
Nincompoop monkeys, good-for-nothing
Ashen-faced puppets – yes, it's natural
Westerners should despise us. They don't know
Japan, nor are they interested. Even if
We should deserve their knowledge and respect,
There would be neither – because they have no time
To know us, eyes to see us . . . Lesser breeds:
We need *improvement* (Brett has told me so),
And Western intermarriage would improve us.
We are the end of something, on the edge.

51

The loneliness, the grieving heart of things,
The emptiness, the solving fate that brings
An answer to the question all men ask,
Solution to the twister and the task.

'Tears welling up in a strange land,
   I watch the sun set in the sea':
Yes, true, but for the sun, which once a week
May sidle itself weakly through pale clouds,
And for the sea, which somewhere – south or east –
Lies far beyond me, and is not my sea.
But tears well up, indeed, in a strange land
And speak of nothing but my lack of speech.
Curt monosyllables jab and jabber on,
Perverted versions of the tongue I know
Or thought I knew – the language Shakespeare spoke,
And Lemuel Gulliver's pure dictions mouthed
By me, alone, in Kanda, Matsuyama,
In Kumamoto . . . sailing through such seas
And on such seas of rhetoric and doubt
Towards these other islands where the sun
Has set before it rises, Ultima Thule,
Where tears well up and freeze on every branch.

I creep into my bed. I hear the wolves.

Remembering Herun-san: 1931

Half-blind, the other eye a livid bulb
Lighting the great beak of his *gaijin* nose
(Even when young, before the Oedipal wound,
'The large alarming eyes of myope') –
And tiny, too, 'mere mite of literature',
Fey Graeco-Irish wanderer in torment
Flinching away from fancied slights and jeers.

His introduction – by-ways of scholarship,
Martinique grammars, Creole dialects,
Mixed with 'artistic labours', Chinese ghosts . . .
His mind inflamed with all things Japanese,
So new, so ancient, fairy-folk who achieve
Delicate miracles on a bowl of rice.
He would live here, record the miracles –
'All the sweet glamours, translucent, milky, soft' –
But needed help, my help: poor amateur,
Keen to impress with learning; doubting; abject.
We found the post in Matsué. He went.

Letter upon letter, following a graph
Of ecstasy, dejection, blankness, rage –
Against 'the shallow-pated missionaries',
Against frock-coated fairy-folk who ape them –
Then soaring up to map his destiny:
'To set minds dreaming, or darkling in new dreams'.

We seldom met; but then, that one 'good' eye
Roved like a moth round everything it saw,
Details distinct, groped-round: the wallpaper,
The backs of books, ornaments, pictures, pots –
He could have made a catalogue of these.
Yet as for the horizon and the stars –
He had never seen them, could not understand
The whole of things, but only part with part.
He lived in books, worshipped the makers of them –
Gautier, Tolstoi, Swinburne, Loti, Kipling,

Joaquin Miller, Sacher-Masoch . . . Then
Feared he knew nothing, ought to curb himself
To birds, cats, insects, flowers, 'queer small things'
(Perhaps himself), leaving the larger themes
To 'men of brains' (myself?). Anxious, inflamed,
Pain working within him, filling his mouth with blood,
Wooing that mighty image-maker, Death,
Seeking its great, sweet, passionless unity.

*　　*　　*

Shy moth, perpetual foreigner, that night
We sat among the hotel's shrubbery shadows
At Miyanoshita, I saw your wings
Flutter and graze the objects you desired
And veered away from: seductive Western things –
Good wine, cigars, deep armchairs, play of mind
Following logic, wit, urbanity,
All that opposes those blind tendencies
You nurtured, desired, feared, subliminal
And startling outward consciousness . . . Romance
Stifled your disappointments, and renewed them;
Faced you with heavenly magic, then withdrew,
Faced you with ignorance – 'to have learned about Japan
Only enough to know . . .' *that you knew nothing*;
Stumbling through language you could but 'pidgin' in
To 'Little Wife', to 'Mamma-San', your toy,
Your shy interpreter of all you knew.
She was your voice, your ears, your oracle
Telling you ghostly stories in a tongue
Invented by the two of you – 'heart-things'.

Eternal restlessness, and joy, and rage –
Japanese angels devils in a wink,
And back again to angels. 'Enemies'
On every side, invented persecutions,
The stridulous telegraphy of critics
Buzzing behind your blinded forehead's dome.

Your 'Mamma-San' recorded what you said
On that September day when your frail heat
Burned itself out at last:
                                        'Never weep
If I should die. Buy for a few sen
A little earthen pot, and bury me
In some small temple yard in some dim place.
Never be sorry'.

Strange impulses, desires, and memories,
Inventing old romance, while all around
The red sun rose, presaging fire and sword,
And fairy-folk went burning through the world . . .

'And I have more, so much much more, to say'.

Great Foreign Writer Visits
Age-Old Temple,
Greeted by Venerable Abbess: 1955

GFW: I am most honoured
to be received here
this afternoon.

VA: We are very glad
that you came
despite the heat.

GFW: I hear there are
many National Treasures
in this temple.

VA: This building is itself
a National Treasure,
as is the Buddha
deified inside it.

GFW: May I ask
how old
the temple is?

VA: This temple
is one thousand four hundred
years old. I am the one hundred
and nineteenth abbess.

GFW: In what dynasty
was the temple founded?

VA: In the era
of the Emperor Kinmei,
when the Buddha came
to Japan . . . May I ask
your purpose in coming
to Japan?

56

GFW: I came to Japan
       to know more about
       the Japanese people
       and Japanese culture,
       of which we know something
       in my country, and admire.

VA: And may I ask how long
       you intend to stay?

GFW: Three weeks.

VA: In regard to religion,
       are you studying Christianity
       or Buddhism primarily?

GFW: I am interested in all religions
       as a form of man's behaviour.

VA: Is this your first
       visit to Japan?

GFW: Yes, but I have known
       Japanese history
       Japanese art
       and Japanese literature
       a long time.

VA: I feel very much assured
       that you have so much understanding
       towards these things.

GFW: Thank you very much.
       I wish more people from my country
       could know your people
       and your country.

57

VA: Can you eat
        this kind of
        Japanese cake?

GFW: I am sure I can
        because I like
        all Japanese food.

VA: Are you giving a lecture
        or something?

GFW: I am attending a seminar
        on our country's literature.

VA: It must be very trying
        in this hot season.

GFW: No, this season
        is like the season at my home –
        very pleasant.

VA: Have you a message
        for our youth? For the world?
        What is your impression
        of our women? Of God?
        May I ask
        what tobacco you smoke?

GFW: To thine own self be true.
        May peace prevail.
        Very beautiful.
        The same to all but
        called by different names.
        A blend I have made up.

VA:	Thank you very much for coming.
GFW:	Thank you for all your trouble.
TOGETHER:	Thank you. Thank you. Thank you.
GFW:	*Arigato* . . . (Did I get that right?)

Notes to 'Voices Through Clouds'

Kirishitan Monogatari
Three Last Words: 1620, 1636, 1639

I: Fucan Fabian (also variously known as Fukansai Habian, Fabian Unguio, etc. 1565? – after 1620): the chief Japanese intellectual of the so-called 'Christian Century' (1549–1650), he was converted to Christianity about 1583, admitted to the Society of Jesus as lay brother in 1586, rose as teacher in the Jesuit *collegio* in Amakusa, and achieved notoriety as preacher and as polemicist against Buddhism, Confucianism and Shinto. He abandoned the Jesuits about 1608, and by 1618 was actively engaged in the persecution of Christians in Nagasaki. In 1620 he wrote *Ha Daisu* ('Deus Destroyed'), a refutation of Christianity which mirrors and perverts many of the intellectual objections he had earlier made to the accepted faiths of Japan.

II: Among Fabian's chief victims was Fr. Christovão Ferreira, a Portuguese Jesuit who, after prolonged interrogation and torture, apostasised. He became a Zen Buddhist, adopted a Japanese name, Sawano Chuan, and himself became a persecutor of the Christians. However, it is said that later, in the extremity of illness, he renounced his apostasy and died a martyr.

III: *Kirishitan Monogatari* ('Tales of the Christians') is the title of an anonymous chapbook dated 1639, the first of many popular fictional narratives published in the 17th and 18th centuries dealing with early Japanese Christianity. The villains were in general the *Namban* ('Southern Barbarians', i.e. Portuguese and Spanish), and in particular the *Bateren* (Jesuits) and *Furaten* (Franciscan friars).

The poem draws on much material. I must acknowledge many debts to *The Christian Century in Japan* by C. R. Boxer (Stanford, 1951) and to *Deus Destroyed* by George Elison (Harvard, 1973).

Letters from Jakarta: 1641 and 1680

Much the most famous of the *Jagatara-bumi* ('Letters from Jakarta') is in fact a fabrication by a Nagasaki scholar, Joken Nishikawa (1648–1724), drawing on the story of Oharu (1624–97), a girl of mixed Dutch-Japanese parentage who was exiled from Nagasaki to the

Dutch colony of Java by the Tokugawa shogunate's expulsion act of 1639. This poetic lament had wide circulation, is still well known, and is often accepted as authentic. However, some genuine Oharu letters survive, full of prosaic detail, from the years 1672–92. I am indebted to Reiko Yamanouchi for a version of the Nishikawa piece, and to Yoko Okuda and Tomoko Nakagawa for their work on a genuine late letter. The poem draws on both.

On Dejima: 1845

Dejima was the name of the artificial island constructed in Nagasaki harbour by the Tokugawa shogunate between 1634–36. Its 1·3 acres was the only place in Japan where Westerners, first the Portuguese and then the Dutch, were allowed to live from the 1630s until 1856. A short bridge to the north was its sole link with the rest of Japan, and comings and goings were rigidly restricted. In the Dutch period, drawn on here, its inhabitants were mainly the trading-company director, his employees, and some sailors. It is now part of the mainland, but its dimensions and some traces of its buildings can still be seen.

The Envoys: 1860

In 1860, a delegation of 77 officials was sent to the United States by the Tokugawa shogunate, the first of a number of such embassies sent abroad. A diary was kept by one of the envoys, Norimasa Muragaki. This was later published as part of *The First Japanese Embassy to the United States* (The America-Japan Society, Tokyo, 1920). Walt Whitman saw the envoys' arrival in New York: see 'A Broadway Pageant', *Leaves of Grass*, 1867.

Of Japan at Ten Hours' Sight: 1889

Rudyard Kipling visited Japan in March–September 1889. He published an account in *From Sea to Sea: Letters of Travel*, Pt. I (New York, 1900).

Soseki: December 1902

Natsume Soseki (1867–1916), by general consent the leading Japanese novelist of the modern period, began as a scholar of foreign, and in particular English, literature. In 1900 he was sent by the Japanese Ministry of Education to study in England, where he remained until early in 1903. He worked privately in London, taking some tutorials from the Shakespeare scholar W. J. Craig. Towards the end of his time in England, a colleague reported to the Ministry of Education in Tokyo that Soseki was suffering from a nervous breakdown. I am indebted for several details to the curators of the Soseki Collection in the library of Tohoku University, Sendai, and to Hisaaki Yamanouchi. Two lines have been taken from Shimazaki Toson (1872–1943). The poem was first published in *The Times Literary Supplement*, and later in my *Poems 1953–1983*. The present version contains some revisions, in the interests of accuracy, mainly prompted by Kei Koike.

Remembering Herun-san: 1931

Basil Hall Chamberlain (1850–1935), born in England but largely educated in France and Switzerland, first came to Japan in 1873, taught at the Imperial Naval School in Tokyo 1874–82, and became so proficient in the language that he was appointed Professor of Japanese at the Imperial University (later the University of Tokyo) in 1886. He first met Lafcadio Hearn (1850–1904) soon after Hearn's arrival in Japan in 1890: they met several times, in Tokyo and in Miyanoshita, but their friendship is largely recorded in letters (see *The Japanese Letters of Lafcadio Hearn*, edited by Elizabeth Bisland, Boston, 1922; *Letters from Basil Hall Chamberlain to Lafcadio Hearn* and *More Letters from Basil Hall Chamberlain*, edited by Kazuo Koizumi, Tokyo, 1936 and 1937). Chamberlain retired to Geneva in 1911, and died there. 1931 was the year of the so-called 'Manchurian Incident', which eventually led to full-scale war with China, and then Pearl Harbour.

Great Foreign Writer Visits Age-Old Temple, Greeted by Venerable Abbess: 1955

Based on a transcript, 'Interview at Zenkoji Temple', from *Faulkner in Nagano* (Tokyo, 1956).

Part III

Imagine a City

Imagine a city. It is not a city you know.
You approach it either by river or by one of four roads,
Never by air. The river runs through the city.
The roads enter at the four points of the compass.
There are city walls, old ones, now long decayed
But they are still there, bits of a past it once had.

Approach it now (shall we say) by the road from the east.
You can see the ruined gate from a mile away,
And, beyond the gate, towers that may be temples or tombs.
It is evening, and smoke here and there is rising in drifts,
So meals are being prepared, you suppose, in thousands of houses.
There is a smell of roast meat, a succulent odour.

Now enter the city, go through the eastern gate.
Great birds, like vultures, shift on its broken tiles.
The street in front of you is obscured by the setting sun,
A yellow-red ball in a dazzling haze of brilliance.
The paving under your feet is uneven. You stumble,
Clutching a door that leans to your hand as you take it.

And now for the first time you are uneasy.
No one is in the street, or in the side-turnings,
Or leaning out from the windows, or standing in doorways.
The fading sunlight conspires with the drifting smoke,
Yet if there were people here surely you'd see them,
Or, at the least, hear them. But there is silence.

Yet you go on, if only because to go back now
Seems worse – worse (shall we say) than whatever
Might meet you ahead, as the street narrows, and alleys
Flow in hither and thither, a dead-end of tangles
Looping forwards and sideways, neither here nor there, but
    somehow
Changing direction like water wind-caught abruptly.

And there you are, now. You may find the western gate.
It must lie straight ahead, the north to your right,
The south to your left. But where is the river
You heard about (you say) at the beginning?
That is for you to find out, or not to find out.
It may not, in any case, serve as a way of escape.

You imagined a city. It is not a city you know.

Cairo

Sleepless in Cairo, nine floors above the Nile,
The air-conditioning playing castanets,
The caffein twitching at the ends of nerves.
Shrouded in fumes the city roars below.

And at its edge burnt Fustat chokes with dust:
Each footfall, treading, sinks and puffs up dust,
Cones of smashed brick, an avalanche of sherds,
Greased smoke from kilns, dismembered
    pyramids.

A dead dog fans up fast a wedge of stink
That hangs in heat, then falls to a rushed breeze.

Ancestral dregs: such fear encased in power,
Layer upon layer, ebony, silver, gold,
Chariots, sandals, incense, sweetmeats, toys.

The Ramses Hilton rises, catafalque
Above successive cities, holds us here
Shrunk Mamelukes and Pharaohs, side by side –

That frozen mask, magnificent, awake
Night after night, staring at no sky,
Airless in luxury, at its wits' end.

On Alderney

Under the stars' fixed, distant, cold regard,
The lighthouse beams are pulsing, nervous, hard.

Islands are prisons: so are metaphors.
Walk inland from this beach, beyond the shore's
Display of *son et lumière*, and find
A darkness visible, an age defined
In bunkers, towers, concrete under gorse,
Snarls of barbed wire bunched in a fist whose force
Rises through scrub to trip you. All round,
Beneath it all, exiles lie underground:
Thousands of bodies, tortured, starved, hanged, shot,
'The scum of Eastern Europe'. There is not
A beam to light them there. But by the sea
Their ghosts walk through the pulsing flashes, free:

Though light-years of the stars can't drown their agony.

Dredging

They are dredging the stream: the praying-mantis face
Of the nudging shovel goes in, its teeth on edge.
Mud seethes and settles, settles and seeps back.

Tangle of juicy stems, strewn, cut and bleeding:
Their moistures are at one with the cleared stream,
Drop down, uprooted, yellow-petalled, melt.

Jaws grunt and champ, wisps dripping at the mouth,
Fetch up smashed crocks, slashed tyres, knobs of barbed wire
Under the strewn weeds and the welted clods.

And the thunder thuds, the swollen clouds disgorge,
Swelling the channel, neatly grooved, with flood
Superbly tamed, as accurate as rain.

The Dancing Foxes

An early morning walk in Gloucestershire
Twenty-five years ago: the borrowed cottage, then
A rutted track, a gate, a rising copse,
The wind blowing against me, when
Among the trees I reached another gate.

Leaning, at first I saw the distance rather
Than what the morning gave me . . . Straight
In front of me, six feet away, a vixen
Lay in a couch of bracken, muzzle raised
At her two cubs, dancing on their hind paws,
Rapt as their mother's gaze.
Nimbly they moved. Moved and unmoving, we
Watched as they danced, vixen and man content
In what we saw, separately and together.

Until the wind turned suddenly, to scatter
Vixen and cubs across those distances,
Leaving me at the gate among the trees.

Telling Tales

The making of memory – how it tests and twists,
Delving, arranging, covering things over
Till what was so is not, what was is never,
And the seven-year-old bully who gripped you by the wrists,
Burning them Chinese-fashion, is overlaid
With made-up stories, or pretended nightmares:
Or a half-remembered face stares and stares
Riddling your trite account of what you said
Better in the retelling, an audience
Quite taken in by what you chose to say.

No, it was not like that, was not the way
Things happened to fall out. Yet to make sense
You make a fiction, shut the truth away,
And put it all down to experience.

The Bumps

Nettles and hollows, at the end of the Terrace:
'The Bumps', we called it, and it's now I see
It was a waste land. But not waste to me
Then, five or six years old, who found a space
For things to be imagined in. I went
Day after day in search of butterflies,
For grass-snakes, newts, the bones of dinosaurs,
Whatever dreamed-of currency could be spent
On trove of any sort. And ever since
That place was what I wanted, looked for, found
In wastelands here and there, the cast-off dumps
Where things were to be found which no one found
Except myself, focused too narrowly,
Too innocent to know how memory's tricks
Would play a good half-century later on,
Confusing what's been spent, and dead and gone.

Cousin Anne

Did people live like this – stone floors, no books,
A smelly place out back? Not only that –
Was she our cousin, in the family . . . ?
It was a slum. I knew slums were in books,
But they were all in cities, not the Dales,
And not our family. How did they live,
Living like this, with chilly stone, and smells,
And dirty-looking children, and no books?
I didn't ask while I was there: I knew
They wouldn't want me to. But back at home
I asked, 'Does Cousin Anne live in a slum?'
And heard the embarrassed laughter. What was said
To explain it all I can't remember now,
Nor can I now remember why I asked.

Anecdote
(Summer 1943)

Once, it was different.
That much I can remember.
It was sudden, and special; or possibly
I am reconstructing the whole business.
But certainly it was different.

There was a stream, in the summer,
And thick stuff growing on both sides –
That much I can remember,
And that it was different,
Certainly different,

From any other stream,
Any other summer,
With the stuff quite distinct in its growing
From other stuff.
Hotter, yes, and the stream itself

Warmer than water is now
Unless you actually boil it.
We walked along the stream,
And now I remember the pebbles were hard
Under my feet, if not under hers.

After that, it's hard
To say anything much about it.
Unless I begin lying
Or somehow, anyway, disguising
The thing that it certainly was

And how different, once.

The Play's the Thing

This play is not the truth: it is a play.
My daughter watches it, and tells me so.
It is a play. In 1633
Someone invented it, and wrote it down.
Now, in the present, we sit down and watch
This playing truth, or truthful play, and say
It is not true. Such words, such blood, are not
True to our knowledge, or our sense of what
We know as truth.
             And then we go to bed,
Disturbed by untruth, or by what was said
Closely enough to truth to make us lie
Awake in troubledness, and then to drown
In dreams where no door opens, every latch
Locks at our hand, and all things falsify.

Commination

Words failed him: the dead locution
Apt for once, an epitaph.
Laborious the heavy, tense construction
That casts its shadow like a monolith.

Across the flat acres the rubbled walls
Inhabited by thick-edged clods, blown seed,
Display vermin lodged as empty vessels
Warning us off, consumed, common indeed

In a landscape given over to other cares
Than tribal punishments enacted once.
Cornered, the blunt and humbled church prepares
For Lent, absence and chill penitence.

Here he, and others, died, speaking a tongue
Grotesque to ears unwilling to be cheered
By such small mercies. The wind had a song
Carrying threatening words; dropped; disappeared.

A Set of Metaphors

This frame that feels itself, without desire;
This jointed bonework aching at its joints;
This cavity catching the touch of fire;
This skin a brick wall crumbling, lacking points.

The propped-up dwelling poised to hit the ground;
The vehicle abandoned, obsolete;
The temporary structure, now unsound;
The scaffolding collapsing in the street.

An amplitude that stirs, slow with disuse;
A withering of the thin contagious breath;
A drying wind; a slackening of juice;
A portioning-out of rations against death.

And so much more than each sly metaphor
And so much less to come than went before.

Forgetting

The glasses left at last night's restaurant.
The raincoat in the alcove where you hung it.
The bag you knew you had when you reached London.
The muddle about the name of the booked garage.
The confusion over a number, an address.

What you perhaps said, or might have said.
What comes back later, laughed at by a friend.
What's scribbled in the last page of your diary.
What surfaces next day at 5.0 p.m.
What wakes you from a dream, and is still bad.

Missing, as the ratchet slips on the motor-mower.
Missing, like a tooth the tongue can't leave alone.
Missing, a gap between familiar houses.
Missing, a beat of the heart in fear or exhaustion.
Missing, as in a battle, but not presumed dead.

Worried

One about liver condition, noted by doctors
Giving him four or five months, possibly longer.
One about mortgage-repayments; one about body-smell;
Another who wakes at dawn drugged with psephology,
Recking boundary-changes.

Some with the death of the elm, or the whale, or the planet;
Those who go out with petitions, long-time committee-sitters.
Dreaders of final exams or boards of selection,
Of being found out in adultery, or peculation,
Or organ deficiency.

Others with mothers, too old to be told what is proper,
Or with children who, now far away, are bad correspondents,
Or with colleagues who chatter too much, or too little, or dreamers
Who find their dreams true too often, disaster-prophets,
Hoarders of omens.

All of them gripped by pain, boding, guilt, the inferior furies,
All of them monomaniac in ailment,
All unhelped by spilling the beans, in surgery or confessional,
All obsessed with a thing that is possibly nameless
Or, if named, incurable.

Two Poets*

One is asleep, one dead. Both lie inclined
Towards us, who are awake and still alive.
One's work is over, torn and discarded scraps
Strewn by his elbow. One's is yet to come,
A childlike promise hovering in the trees.

An attic above London, where the dawn
Peers at the burnt-out candle and the boy,
Finished with faking, stretched out on the bed.
A rural toyset static as a dream,
Where horse and pig and poet share the green.

The trees come closer. London vanishes.
The dream is taking over from the toys,
Breaking the promises, poised now to invade
That farmyard round which Russia stretches out
Endlessly, beyond livid smoky clouds.

* *Chatterton* (Henry Wallis, 1855–56)
  The Poet Reclining (Marc Chagall, 1915)

'The anaesthetic from which none come round'

Now what you feared so long has got you too.
The blankness has descended where you lie
Deep in that building you already knew,
And nothing reaches you in vacancy.
Toads and hired boxes all pushed to one side,
Lugubrious jokes made serious at last
There in the loneliest, cruellest, final place,
Your turning over of the wasted past
Has stopped forever. And you meet full-face
The shot that's never missed or fallen wide.

The Mole at Kilpeck Church
(for Geoffrey Grigson)

Fierce kicks and thrustings under turf and leaf
Reveal you, revenant,
Still lively under so much buried grief,
So ready to be quick when all are dead,
So plucky in extending your dark head
Among the carvings of the lost and spent.

Even that famous randy lady who,
Spreading her swollen thighs,
Enacts in stone the acts that we would do,
Seems nothing to your rushing push, your flair
For room to breathe when all the churchyard air
Shrinks to a mere frame for your energies.

Second After Trinity
(for Norman Nicholson)

Nine in the congregation. A clergyman
Who's filling in this Sunday: Austrian, Pole,
Some accent I can't place. Why is he here
(Our usual's off, I know: he told us last
Sunday – trivial details lost in church),
But why this foreigner, whose voice is stranger
Even than 1662? But then, there follows
The question, *Why are we here?*, who duly follow
This staid, familiar, dignified, dead rite.
The ritual itself takes over, just;
And unaccompanied (the organ's off)
We sing two hymns we know but don't quite know,
And speak the words, and slowly up the aisle
Follow the other seven who have come,
Knowing they must, with questions of their own.

Cold Comforts
(for John Betjeman)

What is it to grow old? Matthew Arnold

It is to know that what may just survive
Is nothing but a footnote in a vast
Compendium in 2005,
Bought by five libraries which keep the Past
Locked in a cellar for the literate.

It is to see one's face familiar, but
Changed in a way one did not hope to see:
The eyes too shifty, and the mouth too slack.
It is to alter into vacancy,
Not looking forward, frightened to look back.

It is to wander down that much-trod track
Which leads to private groans and oaths and sighs,
Muttering to oneself a name or two,
Remembering a face, or breasts, or thighs,
How many of them, and yet now how few.

And all of these are known, and all are true,
And none of them gives comfort or relief.
If we could try the whole thing once again,
Would they be different? O the blank belief
That everything is so, and all things vain.

For Roy Fuller at Seventy

A Fuller on the shelf: 'the image noted',
Though whether Roy or John I cannot say
Until I put my specs on. What I've quoted
Is Roy's, of course, and the three words convey

The antiseptic note I find so cheering
Among the dank piles of the verse that comes
(With truculent letters, or, much worse, the leering
Bonhomous scrawls accompanying the Glums)

Onto my desk, or thumping on the mat
Here at the Mill House. You keep up the standards
Old X, young Y, have trampled till they're flat —
Ungolden Oldies or sleek Standard Vanguards

Praised by the ignorant or the tin-eared trendies
Who tell us what is what, and week by week
Build their snug houses frail as Barrie's Wendy's —
The vain, the mad, the stupid, and the chic.

Dear Roy, these quatrains are, I know, splenetic,
Not quite the thing to send on Feb 11.
Past fifty, is the New always emetic?
At seventy, perhaps one thinks of Heaven —

A polished harp, a due reward, a choir
Singing in harmony one's better lines . . .
Below, the ceaseless unremitting fire
Consuming all the others' dim designs.

You will go on for twenty years or longer,
Giving us more of what we seek from you,
Neater and sweeter, crisper, darker, stronger;
Here's to *Collected*, 2002.

A Sort of Ballade for a Sort of New Hero
(for Craig Raine)

Who speaks of Foxall now? In what dark grove
Sits Ketton-Cremer plucking at his lyre?
Where are the followers of Titterton
William Kean Seymour put among the choir
Of heavenly minstrels? And where Fredegond Shove?
Their reputations shrouded, vanished, gone.
There is but one now whom the Muses deign
To set within the pantheon: Craig Raine.

The harp of Humbert Wolfe is quite unstrung,
And Stephen Phillips – that almighty voice –
Is heard no more. The elegiac Rook
Whose Dunkirk verses once resolved our choice
To stand firm on the brink when we were young –
No longer mentioned; he whose metres shook
The heavens, William Watson – sought in vain.
Our single talent's well employed with Raine.

Ask you for Gerald Gould? His tongue is mute,
Like that of Redwood Anderson and Trench,
Fine bards whose promise burst upon the world
But yesterday. The fire that none could quench –
Theodore Maynard – has mislaid his lute.
J. D. C. Pellow, whose great stanzas hurled
Defiance at the night, won't come again.
Our only hope lies now with one: Craig Raine.

Prince, when the slughorn trembles at your lips
Calling disconsolate for Carman, Shanks,
Snaith, Kirke White, Luce, at that apocalypse
When for forgotten poets we give thanks,
Hold firm the note, prolong the dying strain,
Yet is there bounty: we still have Craig Raine.